First World War
and Army of Occupation
War Diary
France, Belgium and Germany

40 DIVISION
119 Infantry Brigade,
Brigade Trench Mortar Battery
25 June 1916 - 31 August 1916

WO95/2607/5

The Naval & Military Press Ltd
www.nmarchive.com
Published in association with The National Archives

Published by

The Naval & Military Press Ltd

Unit 10 Ridgewood Industrial Park,

Uckfield, East Sussex,

TN22 5QE England

Tel: +44 (0) 1825 749494

www.naval-military-press.com

www.nmarchive.com

This diary has been reprinted in facsimile from the original. Any imperfections are inevitably reproduced and the quality may fall short of modern type and cartographic standards.

© Crown Copyright
Images reproduced by permission of The National Archives, London, England, 2015.

Contents

Document type	Place/Title	Date From	Date To
Heading	WO95/2607/5		
Heading	Trench Mortar Battery Jun-Aug 1916		
War Diary	Marles Les Mines	25/06/1916	04/07/1916
War Diary	Les Brebis	05/07/1916	27/07/1916
War Diary	Calonne	28/07/1916	31/07/1916
War Diary	Les Brebis On The Line At Colonne	07/08/1916	07/08/1916
War Diary	Colonne Sector	08/08/1916	15/08/1916
War Diary	Les Brebis	16/08/1916	23/08/1916
War Diary	Loos	24/08/1916	31/08/1916

washroom 9/26/075

40TH DIVISION
119TH INFY BDE

TRENCH MORTAR BATTERY

JUN - AUG 1916

Army Form C. 2118

5/10/244

119th Brigade Trench Mortar Battery

Vol I

WAR DIARY
or
INTELLIGENCE SUMMARY

(Erase heading not required.)

Instructions regarding War Diaries and Intelligence Summaries are contained in F.S. Regs., Part II. and the Staff Manual respectively. Title Pages will be prepared in manuscript.

Place	Date	Hour	Summary of Events and Information	Remarks and references to Appendices
Morles les Mines	June 25th 1916		The Battery assembled here; personnel being drawn from Battalions forming the Brigade.	
	26th		Men's kit had found to be overcrowded, and an additional one found. We took over today eight complete 3" Stokes Mortars, and other stores.	
	27th 28th 29th 30th July 1st 2nd		This week has been occupied in instructing the men in the advanced stages of the use of the Mortars; gun drills &c; also in seeing to the completion of kit and equipment. Divisional Ammunition Store Rook practice made with firing three shells (unfused) as dummies for purposes of instruction. Three boxes of "Stokes" shells have been obtained from	
	On the 28th		Capt. Montgomery took command of the Battery.	
	3rd		Battery ordered to proceed to the line. Moved from Morles to Observations (near Bordin) and spent the night in bivouacs. Attached to Machine Gun Coy for rations.	
	4th		Battery proceeded to Les Brebis and took over the Billets of 1st French Mortar Battery. The right half Battery with Lieut. Thomas + 2nd Lt. Jones proceeded to Colonne Station & took over the six gun stations of the outgoing Battery.	
Les Brebis	5th		Situation in the 2nd quiet, and nothing of consequence reported.	
	6th		Enemy quiet. Necessary to considerably alter the arrangements of No 4 gun at present, as it is so arranged that proper cartridges obtained + satisfactory regulation needed.	
	7th		Situation quiet.	
	8th		Left half Battery relieved right half, who came out for rest. 2nd Lt. E.A. Robinson (RFA Welsh) reported for instruction + went in with left half Battery.	
	9th		During the night our guns participated with Artillery + heavier Mortars in a bombardment of the Enemy Line in "Wellmany" to a proposed raid by our Infantry.	

1875 Wt. W593/826 1,000,000 4/15 (J.B.C. & A.) A.D.S.S./Forms/C. 2118.

Army Form C. 2118

WAR DIARY
or
INTELLIGENCE SUMMARY
(Erase heading not required.)

Instructions regarding War Diaries and Intelligence Summaries are contained in F. S. Regs., Part II. and the Staff Manual respectively. Title Pages will be prepared in manuscript.

Place	Date	Hour	Summary of Events and Information	Remarks and references to Appendices
Les Brebis	1916 July 10th		Situation quiet. Our bombardment appears to have damaged their wire in places. Nothing of note to record. Our working parties invented no fire from firing much during the hours of darkness.	
	11th		Enemy used shrapnel on right of Brigade front. Our No. 1 & 2 guns opened in retaliation. Corporal Hughes (19 R.W.F.) at No. 2 gun admitted to hospital with shrapnel wound in head.	
	12th		Right half Battery relieved left half. Battery was today transferred from M.G. Co. to Brigade. 2 M. left for rations. Situation quiet.	
	13th		Quiet all day. At about midnight, however, enemy sent over some heavy mortar shells, directly opposite centre of our line. We at once gave him 10 rounds rapid from four of our mortars. He ceased fire.	
	14th		But for a few shells over on Tamworth Trench the night, the situation has been fairly quiet. Whilst going from dug-out in No. 2 gun. Pte. E. Leadbeater (12 S.W.B.) was severely wounded in head by a splinter from a H.E. shell.	
	15th		Inter-Battery relief today. But for a few heavy mortar shells, the enemy has been quiet today. Early in the evening, during the blooming of these completed by us, we shelled the enemy front line & support trenches.	
	16th		Early this morning we participated with the Artillery in heavy French mortars in a bombardment of enemy lines opposite our right. Quiet during the day. We improved our ammunition store at No. 4 gun.	
	17th			
	18th		Quiet during the day. We brought No. 2 gun to bear with good effect on enemy's line opposite Tickle Corner.	

Army Form C. 2118

WAR DIARY
or
INTELLIGENCE SUMMARY
(Erase heading not required.)

Instructions regarding War Diaries and Intelligence Summaries are contained in F. S. Regs., Part II. and the Staff Manual respectively. Title Pages will be prepared in manuscript.

Place	Date	Hour	Summary of Events and Information	Remarks and references to Appendices
La Brebis	1916 July 19th		During this morning, the enemy sent over shells of various calibre on our left, who joined in retaliating & thus caused much damage, however, during this ceased from observation our No. 2 gun seems to have damaged the enemy trenches & were yearning.	
	20th		Inter-battery relief today. Enemy artillery rather active at periods during day and night. We have trench mortars here well in return.	
	21st		We were relieved today by the 120th T.M.B. & proceeded back to billets for a rest.	
	22nd 23rd 24th 25th 26th 27th		Battery employed in cleaning guns and equipment, physical drill, arms drill, etc. Also instruction given in the construction of mortar emplacements and suitable shell proof dug-outs for ammunition to. We have also been able to obtain from the Battalion new clothing & boots for those of our Battery who needed replacements. On 25th Pte. Hill (19th R.W.F.) was admitted to Hospital with Jernia.	
Calonne	28th		Guns were taken up to Calonne by road after dark ready to take over the line again from the 120th T.M.B. 2nd Lt. Robinson returns to Battalion & 2nd Lt. R.D. Davies (18th Welsh) in his place.	
	29th		Right Half Battery relieved 120th. In addition to the original positions, we installed a 4th mortar in Bryan 7 on the left in consequence of increased Brigade frontage.	
	30th		Enemy very active with artillery but does not use many light trench mortars. Corporal Hughes discharged from Hospital & returned to duty.	
	31st		With the exception of a few light shells & heavy mortars, the enemy has been quiet today.	

A.G. Montgomery Capt
O/C 119th M.T.M.B.

Army Form C. 2118

WAR DIARY or INTELLIGENCE SUMMARY

119th Brigade Trench Mortar Battery

Vol 2

(Erase heading not required.)

Place	Date	Hour	Summary of Events and Information	Remarks and references to Appendices
La Brique (In the line at Boesinghe)	1916 Aug 1st		With the exception of some rifle grenades & mortar shells which have come over on different parts of the line at varying times, the situation has been fairly quiet. Our firing last night has been somewhat restricted owing to our working parties being after Colonne Secto. (especially on the right) were subjected to a very heavy bombardment. Our guns joined in the retaliation. Jnr. Battery Relief.	
	2nd		The 3rd Division (12th S. W.B.) one of the men on No. 2 gun was shot through the arm whilst observing the firing of his gun. During our relief Pte Ratcliffe was turned by a shell on the parapet. He was going up to No 4 gun with the relief, but being badly shaken though unhurt he was sent back to billets for a rest.	
	3rd		Fairly quiet today but for a little uncommunicate shelling along the front the usual attention by hostile mortars to Butterfly Walk region. Heard today that Pte L. Leadbeater had died of wounds. He had astrafe at midnight with our guns — Fritz became rather excited. Enemy sent over all sorts of stuff by our No. 1 & 2 guns this morning, damaging the trenches by the battery gun.	
	4th		Our two guns on the left joined in a little demonstration by a company of the 12th A.W.R. early this morning. Hun became very nervy. Our No. 4 gun put a little M.G. out with rapid fire.	
	5th		Usual trench mortaring in Butterfly Walk. One of a working party near our No 3 guns was killed & two more & five hostile shrapnel shells dropped into parts of Colonne at unduly touched.	
	6th		Situation normal. Pte P. Leadbeater shot himself through the foot when cleaning his rifle. Jnr. Battery Relief.	
	7th		Enemy rather active with rifle grenades & mortars. We have warned him all day with our guns. The shot from No.2 gun on two gun causes a large explosion in his line.	

1875 Wt. W593/826 1,000,000 4/15 J.B.C. & A. A.D.S.S./Forms/C.2118.

Army Form C. 2118

Instructions regarding War Diaries and Intelligence Summaries are contained in F.S. Regs., Part II. and the Staff Manual respectively. Title Pages will be prepared in manuscript.

WAR DIARY
or
INTELLIGENCE SUMMARY

(Erase heading not required.)

Place	Date	Hour	Summary of Events and Information	Remarks and references to Appendices
Lorette Ridge	14/16 Aug 8th		Enemy fairly active; he shelled our support line rampart on the left for several minutes during the morning. Offensive situation normal.	
	9th		Enemy again active on the left with small calibre shells & rifle grenades. We are sending our Nos 4 & 5 T.M. guns as much as possible, which has very likely drawn his attention to that part of the line.	
	10th		Enemy rather quieter today. We gave him over 100 shells from our guns on the left, but his retaliation was weaker today. No 6 gun hurled over 120 lb. Bgh. in consequence fair frontage being shortened. Inter-Battery relief today. Situation quiet today.	
	11th		Fairly quiet today, except for a rather heavy trench mortar bombardment on our centre, which lasted for about an hour. We opened on the enemy & sent him over 30 shells from No. 3 Gun. He eventually ceased firing before we did.	
	12th			
	13th		Enemy rather more active today. Two of our ammunition carrying party were slightly wounded by a small shrapnel shell bursting just over our T.M. cellar. In the morning we participated in a bombardment of the hostile lines preparatory to our Infantry carrying out a raid. During the actual raid, we continued rapid firing with our T.M. guns to create a diversion which was successful, judging from the attention we received from his artillery by heavy rifle grenade aerial dart & trench mortars. He has not used our lot entire with T.M. shells today, excepting a short period this morning when he appeared to be searching	
	14th	until noon		
	15th		Situation fairly quiet on night & centre, very little retaliation to our guns. In consequence of no many aerial dart & rifle grenades from the enemy on our left frontage, all T.M's carried out a concentrated bombardment of a particular part of the enemy line from which he appeared	

1875 Wt. W593/826 1,000,000 4/15 J.B.C. & A. A.D.S.S./Forms/C. 2118.

WAR DIARY or INTELLIGENCE SUMMARY

Army Form C. 2118

Place	Date	Hour	Summary of Events and Information	Remarks and references to Appendices
Colonne Loloz	1916 Aug 14th (contd.)		to despatch his missile. We used No. 4 + 5 guns also an additional one which we registered temporarily for the bombardment, which closed half an hour. We very carefully registered during the afternoon. Our Stokes did very well. The Staff Officer for T.M.'s specially commending them. Fritz must have been quiet as he brought his Artillery to bear on our front line & support, using 77m/m & 4.2's. Fortunately he did not make good practice & did no little harm. Whilst serving the temporary gun Pte. Gibbons (18th Welsh) sustained a slight injury to his left hand through a piece of burst cartridge case flying into the gun. Pte. (L.) Dean (19th R.W.F.) admitted to hospital with bullet wound in knee caused through a cartridge being in a brazier over which he was cooking. This happened in a dug-out in Tamworth Trench.	
	15th		Enemy shelled our line on the right this afternoon, damaging the support trench near No. 2 gun. He has however been very much quieter with his shells & rifle grenades lately. We were relieved by the 120th Battery this evening.	
La Bucio	16th 17th 18th 19th 20th 21st 22nd		During this period, the Battery being back in Billets, we have occupied the time in thoroughly overhauling the Guns & cleaning & checking stores & equipment. The men have daily parades for physical drill & bayonet fighting, close order & rifle drill. On the 17th we had attached to us for instruction 2 Officers & 16 men from the Brigade; the object being to form a reserve to fill vacancies in the various T.M. Batteries. The members of the class are keen, & making good progress. Attention is also being paid to the improvement of Billets.	
	23rd		Received orders to relieve the 47th Brigade T.M.B. in the Loos Sector & Right Half Battery went into the line this afternoon, the whole of eight guns being put into positions	

1875 Wt. W 593/826 1,000,000 4/15 I.B.C. & A. A.D.S.S./Forms/C. 2118.

Army Form C. 2118

WAR DIARY
or
INTELLIGENCE SUMMARY
(Erase heading not required.)

Instructions regarding War Diaries and Intelligence Summaries are contained in F.S. Regs., Part II. and the Staff Manual respectively. Title Pages will be prepared in manuscript.

Place	Date 1916 Aug	Hour	Summary of Events and Information	Remarks and references to Appendices
LOOS	24th		We have had a very quiet time in the trenches today, & were able to carry out registration of fire with all of our Mortars. The enemy hardly retaliated at all - Their trenches are not so good as ours at bolverne, there being a lack of cover for the men.	
	25th		Situation again quiet today. We shelled the enemy along the front at different periods, & threw a few trench mortar shells & rifle grenades in retaliation which however caused no damage.	
	26th		During the early morning we shelled the enemy, but received no reply later, however, he shelled us with heavy flight T.M's for about an hour. We opened again at once, & managed to get "it's last word", although it was a very lively exchange of shells, T his mettle was rather heavier than our likes. Having noticed a hostile working party in a cat head or Gordons Crater, we shelled that area, causing the enemy to retreat hastily. It retaliated & a further exchange of shells ensued.	
	27th		Enemy is rather more active with T.M's & rifle grenades & we have been busy all day retaliating to him, & also worrying him at odd times. We at periods during the day kept his front line pretty constantly inter. battery work today to be damaging his front line pretty constantly. Inter. battery work noted.	
	28th		Situation practically the same as yesterday, & nothing worthy to record.	
	29th		Many of Trench mortar activity. We had very heavy rain & rough winds today, with the result that the trenches are in a very bad condition	
	30th		Many of the trenches are in a very bad condition. The enemy are more active than usual during the day, but he retaliated very little. The weather is brighter & we are taking in hand the construction of proper emplacements for our guns & one mills accommodation for ammunition & men.	
	31st		The enemy has been rather active today, & the morning during a lively exchange of T.M. shells on the night Rde. Enquiry (1/2 AWS) & Pte. Ruane (19th RMF) sustained flesh wounds from splinters. It is thought that their wounds are only slight.	

N. Rainford Jones 2nd Lt
for O/c T.M.B.

N. Rainford Jones 2nd Lt
for O/c T.M.B.

[Remarks: Pte. Hartley (12 S.W.B) attached for instruction to one of our guns got slightly & will probably be invalided (illegible) in action]

www.ingramcontent.com/pod-product-compliance
Lightning Source LLC
Chambersburg PA
CBHW081254170426
43191CB00037B/2161